MW01202189

THIS BOOK WILL MAKE YOU AN ARTIST

WRITTEN BY
Ruth Millington

ILLUSTRATED BY
Ellen Surrey

For Freddie and Cleo—Keep
on creating!
R. M.

For Dad—Thank you
for making me an artist.
E. S.

First published 2024 by Nosy Crow Ltd.
Wheat Wharf, 27a Shad Thames,
London, SE1 2XZ, UK

This edition published 2024 by Nosy Crow Inc.
145 Lincoln Road, Lincoln, MA 01773, USA

www.nosycrow.com

ISBN 979-8-88777-042-0

Nosy Crow and associated logos are trademarks
and/or registered trademarks of Nosy Crow Ltd.

Text © Ruth Millington 2024
Illustrations © Ellen Surrey 2024

The right of Ruth Millington to be identified as the author and Ellen Surrey
to be identified as the illustrator of this work has been asserted.

All rights reserved.

This book is sold subject to the condition that it shall not, by way of trade or otherwise,
be lent, hired out, or otherwise circulated in any form of binding or cover other than that in
which it is published. No part of this publication may be reproduced, stored in a retrieval system,
or transmitted in any form or by any means (electronic, mechanical, photocopying, recording,
or otherwise) without the prior written permission of Nosy Crow Ltd.

Library of Congress Catalog Card Number Pending.

Printed in China.

Papers used by Nosy Crow are made from wood
grown in sustainable forests.

1 3 5 7 9 8 6 4 2

CONTENTS

INTRODUCTION

THIS BOOK WILL MAKE YOU AN ARTIST! YES, YOU!

As you turn the pages, you will meet artists from the past and the present, from different countries around the world. Discover painters, performers, sculptors, craftspeople, and mosaic makers, who have all created amazing art.

But how and why did they make huge murals and stone sculptures, intricate mosaics and paintings filled with thousands of tiny dots? Asking questions like these, and finding out the answers, is called art history—not only is it exciting to explore, but it will give you lots of ideas for when you make your own art.

You will discover what inspired all kinds of artists. Some wanted to sketch portraits of interesting people they met, while others loved to paint landscapes of wildflowers or beautiful beaches. Some created pictures of the exciting capital cities they lived in—London, Paris, Beijing—while others illustrated their strange dreams to make magical universes of their own. All artists use their imaginations!

Many important artists have also been inspired by art history—Pablo Picasso once said he liked to "steal" ideas from other artists. So you can steal any of the ideas from this book, too . . .

You are about to learn the secrets of creating great art using different techniques. You may have tried some before, like drawing and painting, but there might be some brand new techniques to try out for the first time. Prepare to be surprised by some of the ways people have made art, from dancing with paint to wrapping shopping carts in string!

You will also discover different styles, which is the way that an artwork looks. Some artists have created their own style, while others have worked in groups, and through movements, to develop a style which they have shared. Art can be big or small, modern or traditional, abstract or realistic. Some of these words might be new to you, but this book is here to teach you the terms and language that artists use!

Most important of all, this book will let you learn about art through making it! After meeting each artist at work, you will be able to use their tips and techniques to paint a still life like Van Gogh, carve a sculpture like Hepworth, create a crown like Basquiat, and much, much more.

Now it's your turn!
Be inspired by this book and become an artist . . .

GETTING STARTED IN YOUR STUDIO

From sitting inside a cozy bedroom to standing on a blustery beach, artists have worked anywhere and everywhere. In this book, you will find Frida Kahlo making self-portraits from her bed in Mexico, and Claude Monet painting in his huge garden—filled with giant waterlilies—in France.

Throughout history, many artists have also worked from a special place called a studio. Inside this space, an artist can experiment on their own, or work with others.

Artists might sketch in small notebooks, paint on enormous canvases hung on the wall, or carve sculptures on the floor. Sometimes an artist will keep their artworks hidden in their studio until they are ready to reveal them to the rest of the world. The studio is the place that art is created so wherever you are can become your studio.

Inside, an artist will usually keep their tools, materials, and any objects of inspiration that they need, including plants and vases of flowers, decorative masks, paint pots, and sharp scissors. What else do you think an artist might keep in their studio?

WHAT WILL YOU NEED TO MAKE ART?

▼▼▼▼▼▼▼▼▼▼▼▼▼▼▼▼▼▼▼▼▼

In this book you will discover a variety of different materials that artists have used—from paper and paint to ribbons, yarn, twigs, and even their own hands and feet—to make art.

For many of the activities in the book you will only need a few items, including lots of things you might be able to find in your home already. However, you will also need some more specialist artist tools and materials like those on this page.

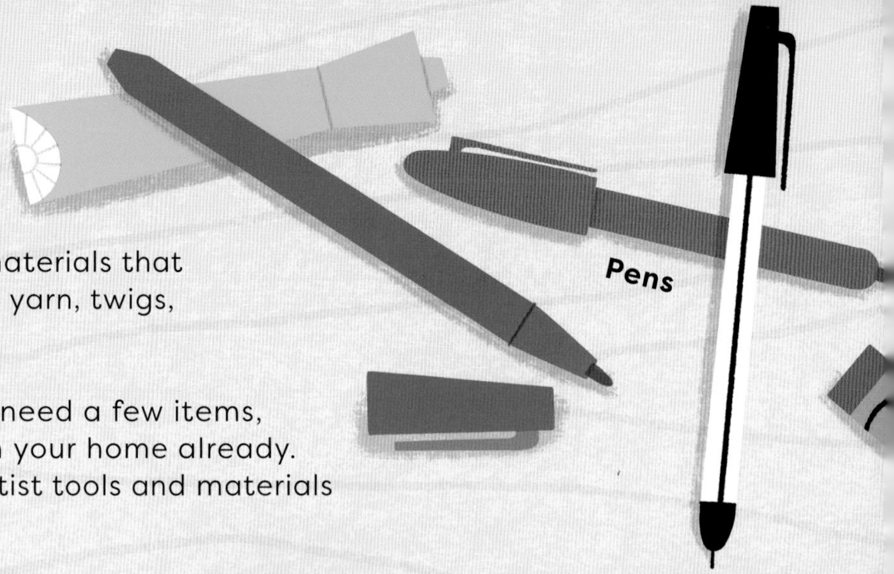

Pens

Some tools and artist materials you might need

Tape

Scissors

Glue

Sticks

Yogurt containers

Pencils

Paintbrushes

A palette

Keeping clean

Making art can be messy sometimes! It's a good idea to have an apron or old T-shirt to cover your clean clothes, and some newspaper and a tablecloth to protect your home.

Different types of paint—watercolor, acrylic, poster, oil

Paper

Cardstock

Your imagination!

The most important thing any artist needs is . . . imagination! You can use anything to make art, and the activities in this book have been designed so you can replace items with others if you don't have them at home. Be as inventive as you like because that is part of being an artist!

PRACTICE, PRACTICE, AND MORE PRACTICE

If you'd like to become an artist, you will need to practice, practice, and practice some more. But don't worry, it's fun! If you play sport or a musical instrument you'll understand that it's important to practice so that you can improve. It's just the same with art—the more you practice your artistic skills, the better an artist you will become.

Warming up!

It's a good idea to warm up before you start making art. Just like a musician might play a warm-up scale before performing an entire song, or a football player will stretch before a game—an artist needs to get ready. When you are warming up, you don't need to have any idea what your artwork will look like. Instead, you can surprise yourself!

THE COLOR WHEEL

To help them, artists often use a color wheel, which organizes colors. There are six colors in this color wheel—red, orange, yellow, green, blue, and purple—and the circle is divided up into slices like a pizza. Three slices are filled with the primary colors: red, yellow, and blue. You can't make any of these colors by mixing others together.

But when you mix two primary colors together, you can create a secondary color: orange, green, or purple. In fact, the color wheel shows you which colors you need to mix together to make each of the secondary colors. Take a look at the color wheel and you'll see that the secondary colors sit in between the two primary colors that make it.

Now it's your turn!

1. Try out making purple, green, and orange! You'll need some paper, a palette, a paintbrush, poster paint, and a jar of water.

TIP: Start by using small amounts of paint and add more if you need to.

If you mix blue and red together, they make purple.

Blue and yellow make green.

Now it's your turn!

With a pen, crayon, or pencil, start in the middle of a piece of paper with a small dot. Now take it on a walk, without taking your hand away from the paper. Want to zigzag up and down, wiggle around, or loop-the-loop with your line? It's up to you! Fill the page with your line, leaving as much or as little space as you like with your continuous line drawing.

2 The color wheel also shows you which colors look good next to one another. Pick a color on the wheel and find the color directly opposite it—that is its complementary color.

3 Choose different pairs of colors and paint small rectangles of these side-by-side on a piece of paper. You can see which colors are complementary, because they make each other stand out.

Red and yellow make orange.

4 Next, experiment by adding more water to your paint. Choose just one color to create another line of rectangles. But, as you paint each rectangle, add slightly more water to your paint, mixing this on your palette first. How does the color change?

Being an artist is all about experimenting—with different colors, dots, lines, water, and many other materials.

This book will give you ideas about what you want to make, and how you can do it. It's okay —actually, it's important—to make mistakes. Some of the most famous masterpieces were the result of happy accidents!

There is no right or wrong in art. But there is one important rule: keep on creating!

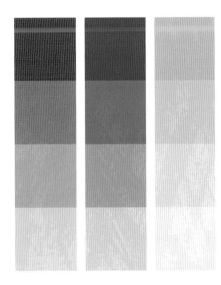

Make handprint art like
A CAVE PAINTER

CAVE PAINTINGS are some of the oldest works of art in the world. They were made many thousands of years ago and have been discovered on the walls and ceilings of caves in countries from France and Spain to Indonesia. Most of these ancient paintings show people and animals, but some even show the handprints of the artists from 40,000 years ago!

Back in prehistoric times, humans used stones and bones to hunt animals and gather food to eat. They also used these tools to make art on the rocky surfaces of the caves they lived in.

They often painted pictures of the animals they hunted, including bulls, deer, rhinos, and woolly mammoths!

To make handprints, people would press their hands flat against the rock, spread their fingers wide, and paint around the edges. They would also press their hands in paint and stamp them against the wall. It's as if they were saying, "I was here."

We can figure out the age of the people who made this art because of the size of their hands—some were children who had tiny hands. Painters also used their fingers, dipped in paint, to draw dots and lines on the cave walls.

Paint was made from ground-down rocks, berries, and even the blood of animals.

This means they only had a few colors, including red and black.

NOW IT'S YOUR TURN!

1 Prepare your ancient paint. For each color add a few heaping teaspoons of a bright spice, such as turmeric, cinnamon, or cumin, to a small cup of white paint. Add a dash of water and pour it onto a paper plate.

What you will need:

* ★ Kitchen spices, e.g. turmeric, cumin, cinnamon
* ★ White paint
* ★ Water
* ★ A paper plate
* ★ Newspaper (to protect the wall)
* ★ Tape
* ★ Brown paper
* ★ And, most importantly, your hands!

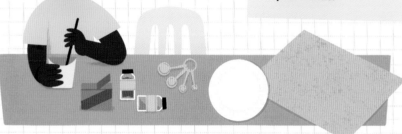

2 Cover a wall in your home or garden with newspaper, taping it firmly in place. Then tape a large piece of brown paper to the middle of the newspaper.

THE DAILY NEWS

3 Press one of your hands into the first color of paint and stamp it against the paper on the wall. Repeat several times in different places and using your different colors. Add as many handprints as you like.

TIP: You could invite friends and family to make handprints too, so you have a mix of shapes and sizes.

13

Make a mosaic like
AN ANCIENT ROMAN

Where do you usually see art on display? Most of the time, you will find art on the wall of a museum, gallery, or your own home. But the ancient Romans could look down and discover art on the floor. Made from lots of tiny little tiles, these types of pictures are called **MOSAICS**.

Some ancient mosaics made almost 2,000 years ago still exist today. Some of the very best examples are in Pompeii, a city in Italy that was destroyed in 79 CE when the volcano Mount Vesuvius erupted and covered everything in ash and lava.

But, hundreds of years later, underneath the lava and ash, explorers discovered mosaics on the floors of houses, swimming baths, and even on the sidewalks around the city.

Ancient Roman mosaic makers showed scenes from everyday life: people wearing togas, their favorite foods and drinks, and animals.

NOW IT'S YOUR TURN!

What you will need:

Colored paper or recycled magazines, greetings cards, tin foil, wallpaper or wrapping paper

Glue

A pencil

Scissors

A piece of thin cardstock

A ruler

1. Choose an animal and draw its outline in the middle of your piece of cardstock.

2. What colors would you like your animal to be? Cut some colored paper into small square tiles.

TIP: Cut the paper into long strips first, then cut the strips into smaller squares. They don't need to be perfect squares—ancient Roman tiles weren't!

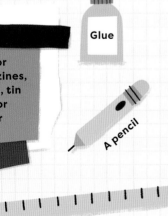

Mosaic makers had to be patient. It took a long time to stick the tiny tiles onto the floor, one by one, using a strong glue. They left a small space between each tile to show the pattern. A pattern is when you use the same shape again and again. Can you see how the mosaic below is made from lines of squares?

At the entrance to one house in Pompeii is a mosaic of a dog, with the words "**CAVE CANEM**," meaning "BEWARE OF THE DOG."

The artist who made this mosaic would have started by creating lots of small tiles, using a hammer to break an old pot into pieces.

A mosaic maker would finish their work by adding a neat border of tiles around the edge to create a picture frame.

3 Decorate your animal by sticking tiles down in repeating rows. It's easier to add glue to a small area of the cardstock then stick tiles onto it, rather than gluing each tile.

TIP: Leave some space in between the tiles so it looks like an ancient Roman floor.

4 For extra details, cut different-shaped tiles and add these into the pattern. Triangle tiles work well for an animal's ears, paws, or tail.

5 Decorate the background by arranging lighter colored tiles in rows.

6 Create a border by sticking darker colored squares in one long line around the edge of your cardstock.

Measure your proportions like
LEONARDO DA VINCI

Leonardo da Vinci was born in Italy in 1452. He is one of the world's most famous painters. But he was also an incredible inventor, mathematician, musician, and scientist. He wasn't only interested in what the world looked like, he also wanted to understand how it worked.

Da Vinci didn't go to school. Instead, his father taught him at home. He was always writing and drawing new ideas in his notebooks, including designs for musical instruments, cars, parachutes, airplanes, and helicopters, many hundreds of years before it was even possible to fly.

Da Vinci also created many drawings of human bodies. This is called anatomy—it's both an art and a science. He realized that the structures beneath the skin are what make you look like you do on the outside!

He liked measuring different parts of the human body. How far down your head do you think your eyes are? Take a look in a mirror and you'll see that they are actually about halfway down your face. Now look at the space between your eyes—this is roughly the same width as an eye. The human body is made up of math!

NOW IT'S YOUR TURN!

It looks like Da Vinci wanted to keep some ideas a secret, because he often wrote them down using back-to-front "mirror writing"—someone would need to hold a mirror up to it to be able to read the words.

Leonardo da Vinci was interested in these measurements because they helped him draw people, including the woman in his most famous painting, the *Mona Lisa*. These rules about the length and distance between parts of the body are called **PROPORTIONS**.

1 Lay your huge piece of paper on the floor and secure the corners with masking tape so that it doesn't move.

2 Lie down on the paper—first with your feet together and arms out to your sides, then in the "star position," with your feet apart and arms raised slightly. In both poses, ask your helper to draw all the way around you with a pencil.

3 Up you go! Now draw a circle around your body. It should touch your raised hands and toes in the drawing.

TIP: To help you draw a perfect circle, tie a piece of string (the same length as your belly button to your toes) to your pencil. Pin one end of the string in the center of the drawing, pull the string tight, and circle the pencil all the way around.

What you will need:

* A huge piece of paper (a roll of brown paper is ideal or you can tape several pieces of paper together. It needs to be bigger than you).
* A helper, to draw around you!
* Masking tape
* A tape measure / ruler
* A pencil
* String
* A pin

TIP: Record your measurements around the edge of the drawing, just like Da Vinci. Try using mirror writing!

4 It's time to get measuring! With a ruler or tape measure, figure out the length of your head. How many times does it fit into your body? Are your outstretched arms the same length as the height of your body? How far down your body is your belly button? Is it in the center of the circle?

5 Now draw some features onto your face. Can you remember how far down the eyes should be? Take a look at yourself in a mirror to see if this is true. Add your eyebrows, ears, nose, and mouth to the drawing.

17

Paint a self-portrait like
ARTEMISIA GENTILESCHI

Artemisia Gentileschi was an Italian painter who worked during the 1600s. We know what she looked like because she used to paint pictures of herself—this type of artwork is called a **SELF-PORTRAIT**.

From the age of 15, Gentileschi sold her paintings to rich Italians. This was unusual, not just because of how young she was, but also because hardly any women were artists. Back then, women were expected to stay at home and look after their children. They weren't allowed to study with men at art schools. Luckily, Gentileschi's father was a great artist. He taught her the skills of painting herself in a realistic way.

To make her self-portraits, Gentileschi would hold a small mirror in her hand, using it to look at closely and then copy the appearance of her face and shoulders. But she also wanted to show something else.

What other object is she holding in her hands? In one, she has a paintbrush and in the other a palette, filled with different paint colors. She included these details in her painting to tell us that she is *an artist*.

Gentileschi was showing people that women could be artists too. But learning to paint was hard work and you can see this in her self-portrait. Her hair is untidy and there is sweat on her forehead as she leans in to paint her picture, focusing on the important task ahead.

What do you think Gentileschi is thinking or feeling? She isn't smiling, and that's because she wanted to present herself as a serious painter, just like her father.

NOW IT'S YOUR TURN!

What you will need:

A palette or a paper plate

Poster paint

A mirror, ideally a small one that you can hold in your hand

A paintbrush

A piece of paper

A pencil

1 Look closely at the reflection of your face in a mirror. What makes you special? What shape is your head? How big are your eyes? Spend some time looking at yourself carefully before you start drawing.

2 Use a pencil to draw the outline of your face onto the center of your paper. Then draw your shoulders. Leave space around the edges, since you will use this later.

3 Now draw in the details, like your hair, ears, nose, and eyes. Do you look serious like Gentileschi or are you having fun? Are you smiling or frowning?

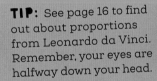

TIP: See page 16 to find out about proportions from Leonardo da Vinci. Remember, your eyes are halfway down your head.

4 Next it's time to show that you are an artist! Draw the objects you're using around the edge of your self-portrait—you can even draw the mirror that you're using to look in.

TIP: To make sure your self-portrait looks like you, try to use the same colors that you can see in the mirror.

5 Now you can begin painting. Start with your hair and work from the top of the paper to the bottom, so you don't smudge your work.

6 What does the room around you look like? What color are the walls? Add these colors around yourself to complete your self-portrait as an artist at work.

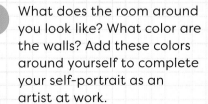

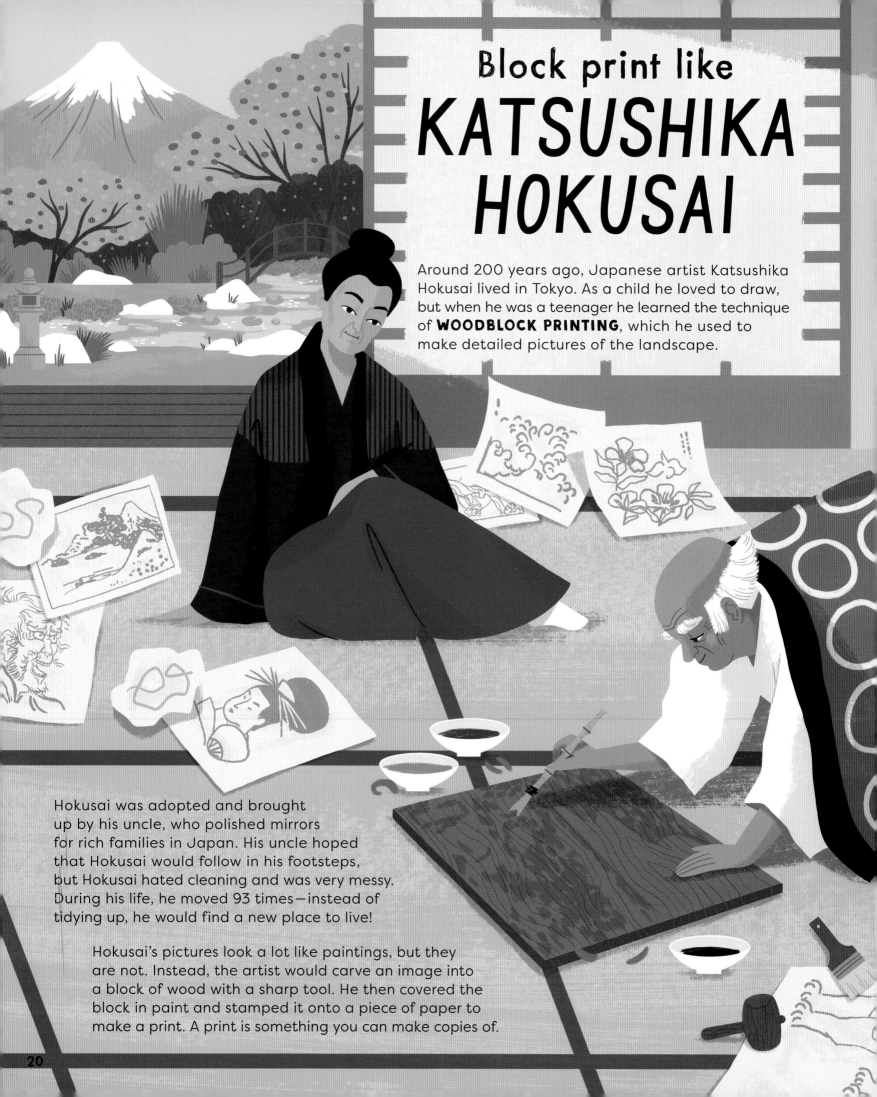

Block print like
KATSUSHIKA HOKUSAI

Around 200 years ago, Japanese artist Katsushika Hokusai lived in Tokyo. As a child he loved to draw, but when he was a teenager he learned the technique of **WOODBLOCK PRINTING**, which he used to make detailed pictures of the landscape.

Hokusai was adopted and brought up by his uncle, who polished mirrors for rich families in Japan. His uncle hoped that Hokusai would follow in his footsteps, but Hokusai hated cleaning and was very messy. During his life, he moved 93 times—instead of tidying up, he would find a new place to live!

Hokusai's pictures look a lot like paintings, but they are not. Instead, the artist would carve an image into a block of wood with a sharp tool. He then covered the block in paint and stamped it onto a piece of paper to make a print. A print is something you can make copies of.

NOW IT'S YOUR TURN!
▼▼▼▼▼▼▼

What you will need:

* A teabag
* A bowl
* Hot water
* A paintbrush
* A white piece of paper
* A piece of cardboard
* A pencil
* String or yarn
* Craft glue
* Blue paint

1 Ask a grown-up to pour boiling water over a teabag in the bowl and let it sit for five minutes.

2 Brush the tea onto your white piece of paper and let it dry.

TIP: You could stain several pieces of paper so you can make more prints.

3 Draw the outline of a big wave on a piece of cardboard with your pencil. Then add in the outlines of several smaller waves in the foreground.

4 Paint over the lines of your drawing with glue, using a paintbrush. Now stick thick string or yarn down on these lines.

5 With your paintbrush, carefully cover only the string with blue paint.

6 You're ready to block print! Stamp your string relief art onto a piece of tea-stained paper, pressing down firmly and then lifting it away carefully.

TIP: Work quickly with the paint so it doesn't dry before you can make your print.

Hokusai often included people in his images. They always look tiny compared to the natural landscape and powerful weather.

Many of Hokusai's prints show the landscape of Japan, including the country's tallest mountain, Mount Fuji. Since Japan is surrounded by the sea, Hokusai often printed the huge crashing waves of the ocean, including one he called *The Great Wave*.

Cut out a silhouette portrait like
MOSES WILLIAMS

Today, it's easy to use a camera to take quick photographs of people. But, back in the 1700s, photography had not been invented yet. So, how could people create pictures to show what a person looked like? African-American artist Moses Williams had a special way of making black and white portraits, called **SILHOUETTE CUT-OUTS**.

Williams started his life as an enslaved man. His enslaver was a man named Charles Willson Peale, who owned a grand museum in Pennsylvania. Museums were usually filled with paintings, skeletons, or fossils, but many Americans visited Peale's museum for a very different reason. Williams, who worked for Peale at the museum, would create their portrait.

He used a machine called a physionotrace, which had a pencil attached to a needle. Visitors would sit in front of the machine, while Williams used it to draw the exact outline of their head and shoulders onto black paper in just a few minutes.

Williams asked people to turn their head and shoulders away from him. When people are looking to one side like this, it makes their features stand out. This view of a person is called "in profile."

A silhouette is when a line is drawn around an object, person, animal, or scene and it's filled with a single color. Your shadow is a type of silhouette.

Williams would then carefully cut around the drawing to create a silhouette. He stuck the silhouettes onto pieces of white cardstock, which they could take away and keep forever.

Williams was so talented that people came from all over America to have their silhouettes made by him and, soon, he was freed from slavery to become a full-time artist.

With the money that he earned, Williams eventually got married and bought his own home—which he would not have been able to do as an enslaved man.

NOW IT'S YOUR TURN!

What you will need:

A pencil

Glue

Scissors

Black paper

Cream or white cardstock

1 Who will you draw first? Invite a friend or family member to sit down in front of you. Make sure they're facing sideways, so you can create their silhouette portrait in profile.

2 Draw the outline of their head and shoulders onto a piece of black paper with a thick pencil. Pay attention to the shape of their nose, mouth, chin, and even strands of hair.

3 Cut very carefully around the outline you've drawn. It's easier to move the paper—not the scissors—as you cut.

TIP: If the person you are drawing sits in front of a white wall, it will be easier to see the shape of their outline.

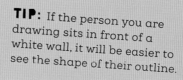

4 Use glue to stick your portrait onto the middle of a piece of cream or white cardstock.

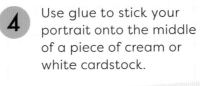

TIP: You can also create a cut-out silhouette using a photograph.

23

Paint outside like CLAUDE MONET

Claude Monet was born in Paris, France in 1840. His father wanted him to help run the family's grocery business but Claude wanted to be an artist. In 1883, he moved to the village of Giverny, about 50 miles from the city, where he created a huge garden by digging, weeding, and planting colorful flowers.

Monet noticed that on a sunny day a field of grass looked bright green. But, during a storm, it turned a deeper, darker shade, like an emerald. He liked the way that weather changes the color of a landscape and wanted to show this in his paintings. He decided the best way to do this was by painting *en plein air*, which means "in the open air."

NOW IT'S YOUR TURN!

What you will need:

A palette or paper plate

Paper towels

Drawing board/clips to hold your painting in place

Poster paint

A jar of water

A blanket or something to sit on

A pencil

A paintbrush

Paper

1 Find an interesting location outside—this could be a favorite spot in your garden or local park. Make yourself comfortable; you might want to sit on a rug while you paint!

2 What's in your view? Are there any flowers? Can you spot a tree? Using a pencil, draw these onto your paper. Don't worry about including lots of detail, you're just adding a few important outlines so you know where to put your paint.

3 Look ahead—is it sunny and bright or a cloudy day? In your view what colors do you see? On your palette add a small splotch of paint in every color that you see. You might need to mix your paint to create some new colors.

TIP: If you add white to a color it makes it lighter.

Taking his easel and paint with him, Monet would choose a spot he liked—a lake, a pretty garden, or a field full of large trees. Painting directly from nature, Monet worked quickly. He had to capture the weather before it changed.

Monet loved to paint the landscape and was also interested in every type of weather: sunshine and rain, wind and snow, rainbows and clouds.

It was a sunny day, so Monet used bright, happy colors: pastel pink and light yellow and white. What other colors do you see?

Also look at how Monet painted the picture with lots of little brushstrokes. Instead of carefully drawing out details, he used dabs of paint. A flower appears as a spot of yellow and each lily pad is a dot of green. Monet wanted to illustrate his "impression" of the scene. And that's why we call him an **IMPRESSIONIST**.

4 It's time to start painting! What is the main color that stands out from the scene in front of you? Dip your brush into this paint and dab it onto your paper quickly, using lots of little dots.

Instead of focusing on just one bit of your painting, work on all of it, adding your first color everywhere it belongs, from the sky to the ground. You might be surprised to see a color where you don't expect it, like spots of blue in the grass. Copy what you see, even if it seems strange.

5 Clean your brush with water and dry it with paper towels. It's important to do this between each new color you use.

6 What's the next color you notice? Add this to your picture everywhere it appears in your view, using little dots and dabs of paint. Now, move onto your third color, and so on. Include as many colors as you can see—there is no limit!

Remember, this is your impression of the landscape. You can return to this location several times, on days when the weather and colors are different, and paint a whole series of impressionist landscapes, just like Monet.

Paint in points like
GEORGES SEURAT

In the 1880s, French artist Georges Seurat invented a new technique of painting, called **POINTILLISM**. If you look very closely at his art, can you see that it is made up of tiny points of pure colors placed right next to one another?

Seurat was an artist. But he also studied science, including how the eye sees different colors.

NOW IT'S YOUR TURN!

What you will need:

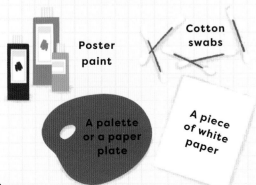

Poster paint

Cotton swabs

A palette or a paper plate

A piece of white paper

1. Add a selection of paint colors to your palette, including brown, green, and blue.

2. First, you need to paint the tree trunk. Take a cotton swab and dip the tip of it into the brown paint. Now, create a vertical line of dots in the center of your paper, leaving small gaps in between your points of color.

TIP: Keep topping your cotton swab up with paint as it runs out.

He realized that if he used small dots of paint, placed side-by-side, they would blur into one image in the eye. This is the same way a computer works: the pixels on the screen are just like the dots in a pointillist painting. Up close, you can see the individual circles of color, but from far away they create a whole picture.

Seurat's pointillist paintings are very vibrant—that's because he chose his colors carefully, using a special diagram called "a color wheel" (see page 10). When Seurat painted using small dots, he discovered special pairs of colors that have a dazzling effect on each other. For example, when he placed green next to red, it made the red stand out more.

Seurat painted his favorite parts of Paris: trees in the park, the winding River Seine, and colorful performers at the circus. He also painted the impressive 984-foot-tall Eiffel Tower the very same year that it was built—in 1889.

3 Add a few branches to your tree, using the dipping and dabbing method with the brown paint.

4 Dip a new cotton swab into your green paint and start to add leaves to your tree, by dotting color around the branches.

5 Using the same green, dot some grass at the bottom of your page.

6 Now, add some flowers to your tree, using a new color. Like Seurat, think about contrasting colors.

7 It's time to fill in the sky behind the tree, using dots of blue. Use dots of yellow in one corner to show the sun shining through, creating a dazzling effect.

TIP: Pointillist painting takes patience. It should take you quite a long time to finish your picture, though probably not years, like some paintings did for Seurat!

Paint a still life like
VINCENT VAN GOGH

Vincent Van Gogh is best known for his paintings of bright yellow sunflowers. Not only are they striking to look at, but they represent how the Dutch artist was *feeling* when he made them.

When Van Gogh lived in the Netherlands, as a young man, he drew pictures of roses, lilacs, and peonies. In 1888, when he was 35, Van Gogh moved to the South of France, where he was excited to find fields filled with sunflowers. He arranged bunches in a vase and began to paint them. This type of artwork is called a **STILL LIFE** because it features objects that don't move.

Van Gogh didn't always copy the objects to look like real life. Instead, he chose colors that showed his emotions, or how he was feeling. Sometimes he struggled with feelings of sadness, but painting bright yellow sunflowers made him feel more cheerful.

The unique style that Van Gogh developed is known as Post-Impressionism.

He used lots of brushstrokes to paint the natural world around him, but he also showed his emotions through bold colors, expressive marks, and thick textures. Making art was a great way for Van Gogh to release his feelings and often helped him feel happier.

Van Gogh's sunflowers almost look like they are moving because of the textured swirling marks.

NOW IT'S YOUR TURN!
▼▼▼▼▼▼▼▼▼▼▼▼▼▼▼▼▼▼▼▼▼▼▼▼

What you will need:

Some flowers and a vase, jar, or container

A flat paintbrush

A thin paintbrush

A piece of matte white cardstock or thick paper (watercolor paper is best)

A palette or a paper plate

A jar of water

Poster paint

Flour

A pencil

1 First, arrange some flowers in a vase, jar, or another container on a table. Move them around until you're happy with how your still life looks.

2 With a pencil, draw the outline of the container and then the horizontal line of the table onto your paper. Now, sketch the flowers, including their petals, stems, and leaves.

3 It's time to paint! But first, how do you feel today? Choose brighter or darker colors depending on your mood. On your palette, mix each color you will need.

TIP: To make thick paint like Van Gogh used, add a teaspoon of flour to each of your colors.

4 Using a flat paintbrush, start by painting the table. Keep changing the direction of your brush as you apply the paint. You want your brushstrokes to be visible. Then wash your brush and paint your background color.

5 Use a thinner brush to paint your flowers, the stems, and the leaves. Start with the center of the flowers and work your way out. Have fun with the paint—your marks don't need to perfect!

6 For a finishing touch, use an even thinner brush to add a dark outline around the sides of the vase and to highlight the edge of the table.

Cut out like
HENRI MATISSE

As a boy, Henri Matisse studied law and in 1888 he began his career as a lawyer in Paris, France. But, four years later, he became ill. While he got better at home, his mother bought him some art supplies. As he started to paint, Matisse realized that he didn't want to be a lawyer anymore; instead, he became an artist for the next 65 years!

When he was in his 80s, he couldn't walk. However, he continued to make art from his wheelchair. He spent most days cutting and sticking down bright pieces of paper onto a flat surface to make colorful **COLLAGES**.

Matisse covered the walls of his home and studio with large cut-outs of fruits, flowers, and plants.

Matisse was a master of making collages. First he would paint huge pieces of paper, each with just one bright color. Then he would cut out the shapes of leaves, birds, and trees. He made the edges as smooth as possible by cutting in one continuous line, without taking his scissors away from the paper. Matisse called this "cutting directly into color" and "drawing with scissors."

Once he had a pile of colorful cut-out shapes, Matisse would place them on a plain piece of paper or canvas. He would move them around many times until he was happy with how they looked. Matisse always left some gaps in between his shapes. This was to make them stand out more. When Matisse was happy with his composition, he would stick down his shapes.

NOW IT'S YOUR TURN!

1 Collect a selection of leaves of different shapes and sizes. You could also pick up other natural objects, such as twigs or flowers.

2 Back at home, lay out your selection of leaves.

What you will need:
* ★ Leaves and/or other natural objects
* ★ Brightly colored paper (or you can use poster paint to make your own, covering several pieces of paper, each with one thick block of color)
* ★ A pencil
* ★ Scissors
* ★ A piece of white cardstock
* ★ Glue

3 Choose your first piece of colored paper. Trace around your first leaf with a pencil. Now place it elsewhere on the paper and trace around it again. Repeat the process several times.

4 Take your next leaf and a different piece of colored paper, repeating the process.

5 Carefully cut out each leaf shape.

6 Next, arrange them onto a piece of white cardstock and when you're happy, stick everything down.

TIP: You could also stick a selection of cut-out leaves to the fridge with magnets.

31

Create a cubist collage like
PABLO PICASSO

Spanish artist Pablo Picasso's artworks are like a jumbled-up jigsaw puzzle. They are made up of jagged and overlapping shapes, different sections, and diagonal lines. This confusing, complicated style is called **CUBISM**.

Picasso was born in the Spanish seaside town of Malaga in 1881. Here he was taught art by his father and his very first word was "pencil." Although he loved Spain, at the age of 23 he decided to move to Paris, France. The city was filled with other artists, photographers, and writers, and Picasso wanted to meet them.

Picasso began to make art that showed the cafés and bars where he made friends with other painters. In many of them it looks like he was standing in different spots around the room when he made them. He liked to look at scenes from above, below, and the sides—all at once. It's as if he had many eyes, including in the back of his head! Picasso broke objects up into different pieces and also included words, such as the name of a drink being served in the bar.

Not everyone liked Picasso's artworks. One writer said the pictures didn't make sense because they were "full of little cubes." This is why we use the word 'cubism' to describe his work.

NOW IT'S YOUR TURN!

Picasso was trying to show us that the world isn't flat. Every object has many sides and Picasso wanted to include them all in his pictures. He didn't just achieve that by painting little cubes; he also made collages.

A collage is an artwork made up of different materials that are glued to a piece of paper or cardstock. In his collages, Picasso would use wallpaper, newspaper, and magazines. He was deliberately adding pieces of the real world to his cubist artworks.

1 Decide on an object that you want to include in your scene. Then cut a selection of newspapers and magazines into squares, rectangles, and triangles of different sizes.

What you will need:

* Scissors
* Collage materials: paper, newspaper, cereal boxes, magazines, old birthday cards, wrapping paper, colored paper
* Three large pieces of colored cardstock
* Glue
* A pencil

2 Stick these to your colored cardstock, starting from the middle and overlapping pieces so they begin to spread outward. Leave some of the colored background visible.

TIP: You could use letters from a magazine/newspaper to spell out special words.

3 Now draw the outline of your object on the cardstock, looking at it from the front.

4 Cut out this outline, then cut it into three or more sections and add to your picture.

5 Now, looking at it from another angle, draw your object on another piece of the same-colored cardstock.

6 Cut this out and then cut it into several sections and add to your picture.

33

Make an abstract mobile like
HILMA AF KLINT

Rather than representing a subject—like a person or landscape—Hilma af Klint preferred to create paintings of colorful circles, spirals, looping lines, and other spinning shapes. She was one of the first **ABSTRACT** artists in Europe.

Born in 1862 in Sweden, Af Klint spent most of her childhood in Karlberg Palace, a military base where her father worked. At the age of 20 she studied art in the capital city, Stockholm, learning to draw and paint. She soon became known for her elegant paintings of people and places and she exhibited her work in galleries.

NOW IT'S YOUR TURN!

What you will need:

A pencil

A sponge

Poster paint

Tin foil

A long piece of string or thread

A palette or paper plate

Scissors

A paper plate

Colored cardstock

Glue

1 Dab your sponge into the paint on your palette and then press it, again and again, onto your paper plate, leaving no white spaces. Let it dry.

But she also began to make abstract art in secret. Af Klint only let a few people see her abstract paintings because she didn't think most people would like or understand them.

Although Af Klint's images are flat and still, many of them look like they are moving because she included swirling shapes in glowing colors. Some of them look like they are made up of flower petals, floating across the surface. They might also make you think of outer space, filled with spinning stars, suns, and orbiting planets.

While Af Klint wasn't interested in painting realistic pictures of the world around her, her abstract art shows how amazed she was by the universe we live in.

2 On pieces of colored cardstock, draw small shapes from Af Klint's paintings—petals, flowers, circles. Cut them out.

TIP: You could decorate the shapes with paint or tin foil before you cut them out.

3 When the painted plate is dry, draw a spiral on it from the outside to the middle. It should look like the shell of a snail that curls inward about three times.

4 Cut along the line until you reach the center, then pull the spiral apart to create a long twist.

5 Glue your smaller shapes to the plate, spacing them out however you like.

6 Poke a small hole in the center of the spiral with the pencil. Thread and tie a piece of string through this and hang it up.

Get surreal like
SALVADOR DALÍ

Spanish artist Salvador Dalí was a **SURREALIST**, which means he didn't want to show the real world in his works. This would have been far too boring for him. Instead, he drew people made of rocks, painted elephants on long stilts, and made the strangest of sculptures, including a lobster placed on top of a black telephone. Dalí's weird and wonderful art never makes any sense!

In fact, Dalí's whole life was surreal. In 1930, he moved into a small house in the fishing village of Cadaqués in Spain. Over the next 40 years, he bought the huts next door, creating a long, winding home, much like a maze. He decorated it with unusual objects and even his pets were peculiar; while most people have a cat or a dog, Dalí owned an anteater.

Dalí would sketch and write down his dreams in a diary so that he could later use them in his art.

Dalí also loved playing fun games, which involved his imagination. He invited other surrealist artists to join him, and his wife Gala, at their house in Spain. One of their favorite games was called "Exquisite Corpse," in which players take turns drawing parts of a human body on a sheet of paper. The result is a shared, surreal creation!

You can see what he dreamed about in his paintings of melting clocks, flying tigers, and a tree growing out of a piano.

NOW IT'S YOUR TURN!

1 Sit in a circle, close enough to pass the piece of paper around but far enough away so you can't see what everyone else has drawn!

What you will need:

* 3 players (or more)
* A piece of paper
* Pencils
* A board or book to lean the paper on as you draw

2 Fold the piece of paper into three equal sections (or more, if there are more players), from the top to the bottom. Now, unfold it to reveal your blank sections to be drawn on.

3 The first player starts by drawing the head and neck of a person in the top section of the piece of paper. Then they fold the paper to hide their contribution.

TIP: Make sure the bottom of the neck just crosses into the second section, so the next player can continue the drawing.

4 The second player takes over and draws from the neck down to the shoulders, arms, chest, and waist. They then fold the paper over, hiding everything but the end of the waist.

5 The third player draws from the waist down to the legs and feet. Once finished, they unfold the entire piece of paper to reveal the surreal "Exquisite Corpse!"

TIP: The stranger your creation, the better a Surrealist you have become!

Decorate your hair with flowers like
■■■ FRIDA KAHLO

In many of her **SELF-PORTRAIT** paintings Frida Kahlo is surrounded by tropical plants, butterflies, birds, and colorful flowers, sometimes even wearing them in her hair. She was celebrating Mexico, the beautiful country where she lived.

In 1925, at the age of 18, Kahlo was badly hurt in a bus accident on her way back from school. She broke many bones and had to recover for several months in bed. During this time she started to paint pictures of herself using a mirror.

Kahlo carried on creating self-portraits throughout her life, painting 55 of them! Even years after the accident, Kahlo's body still hurt, which is perhaps why you won't see her smiling. She used painting to distract herself from the pain. In the courtyard outside her bright blue house, La Casa Azul (The Blue House), she also loved to spend time gardening. Mexico is sunny and has a very hot climate, so Kahlo planted tall palm trees, spiky cacti, and native flowers.

Today you can visit Kahlo's home—she left it as a museum for people from Mexico, and around the world, to enjoy.

If you visited Kahlo in her garden, you might also find some of her pets. She owned two spider monkeys, parakeets, a parrot, an eagle, and a fawn. Sometimes these animals appear in her paintings, sitting on her shoulders or lap.

Kahlo was very proud to be a Mexican woman, which is why she included the country's animals, flowers, and plants in her self-portraits. She also used to wear long, colorful Mexican dresses. It's like she was a walking artwork that celebrated Mexico.

NOW IT'S YOUR TURN!

What you will need:

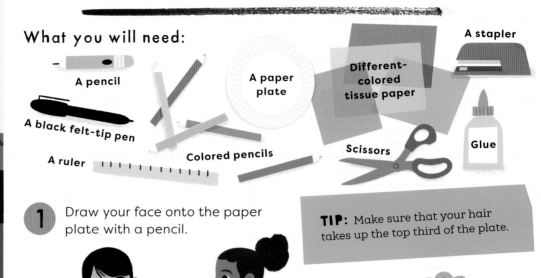

A pencil

A black felt-tip pen

A ruler

Colored pencils

A paper plate

Different-colored tissue paper

Scissors

A stapler

Glue

1 Draw your face onto the paper plate with a pencil.

TIP: Make sure that your hair takes up the top third of the plate.

2 With a black felt-tip pen, color in your hair and carefully go over your features.

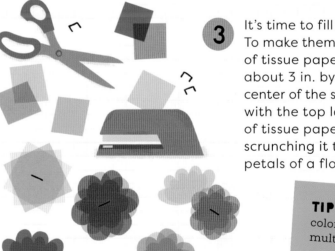

3 It's time to fill your hair with flowers. To make them, cut six layered sheets of tissue paper into small squares about 3 in. by 3 in. Staple the center of the squares. Then, starting with the top layer, pull each piece of tissue paper toward the center, scrunching it tightly to make the petals of a flower.

TIP: You can layer different-colored tissue paper to make multicolored flowers.

4 Once you have a collection of colorful flowers, stick these onto your hair.

TIP: You could also add colorful leaves and butterflies!

Perform a poem like
HUGO BALL

SSSSSHHH! Have you ever visited a museum or art gallery and been told to keep quiet? It's not the kind of place where you're usually allowed to make a lot of noise. But during the 1910s, many artists in Europe did just that. They read out strange poetry and put on loud performances that shocked other visitors.

KARAWANE

jolifanto bambla ô falli bamb
grossiga m'pfa habla horem
égiga goramen
higo bloiko russula huju
hollaka hollala
anlogo bung
blago bung
blago bung
bosso fataka
ü üü ü
schampa wulla wussa ólobo
hej tatta gôrem
eschige zunbada
wulubu ssubudu uluw ssubudu
tumba ba- umf
kusagauma
ba - umf

When the First World War started in 1914, German artist and poet Hugo Ball fled to Switzerland with his wife, Emmy Hennings, who was a singer and dancer. In 1916, they opened a brand-new café called the Cabaret Voltaire, as a place for art, music, poetry, and dance. One evening, Ball stood on stage wearing a funny-looking cardboard cloak and hat. He performed a poem full of made-up words and sounds, which made no sense at all.

NOW IT'S YOUR TURN!
▼▼▼▼▼▼▼

What you will need:

A piece of colored cardstock

Scissors

Glue

A hat or bag

A newspaper or magazine

Colored pens or markers

1 Use your scissors to carefully cut out about 20 words from a newspaper or magazine.

2 Put the words into a bag or hat and shake them up gently.

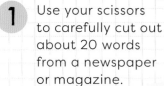

3 Pull the words out one-by-one and arrange them on your cardstock in that same order. Stick them down with glue.

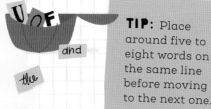

TIP: Place around five to eight words on the same line before moving to the next one.

4 You can use colored pens or markers to create a pattern around or underline the most exciting words to make them stand out.

5 Now it's time to perform your Dada poem in spectacular clothing for your friends, family, or pets! To be as dramatic as the Dada artists, you could make your own unusual costume!

The Swiss artist Sophie Taeuber-Arp would dance to Ball's Dada poems, wearing unusual handmade costumes and masks. She also created wooden puppets to put on Dada puppet shows in galleries.

Ball called this new type of poetry and performance **DADA**. He invented a word that doesn't mean anything but is fun to say out loud. Try it! Other artists, who also moved to Switzerland to escape the war, were soon inspired by Ball's poems and joined him by making their own silly and strange Dada performances.

Romanian artist Tristan Tzara created his own Dada poems to perform. He cut random words out of newspapers, put them into a bag, and jumbled them up. Then, he pulled words out of the bag, one-by-one, and wrote them down in that order.

Carve a sculpture like
BARBARA HEPWORTH

British artist Barbara Hepworth studied **SCULPTURE** in a few different cities—Leeds and London, England, and Florence, Italy. But she was happiest by the seaside. For more than 25 years she lived in a house that was a short walk from the beach in Cornwall, England. On the seashore she discovered pebbles, stones, shells, and caves. She noticed that they were all made up of similar shapes—circles, semicircles, and holes. Inspired, she turned these shapes from nature into large sculptures.

Hepworth was also interested in textures, which is how something feels. A pebble might be smooth, while a rock is rough. Hepworth would often make the same sculpture again and again in different materials such as wood, stone, marble, plaster, and bronze to change its texture.

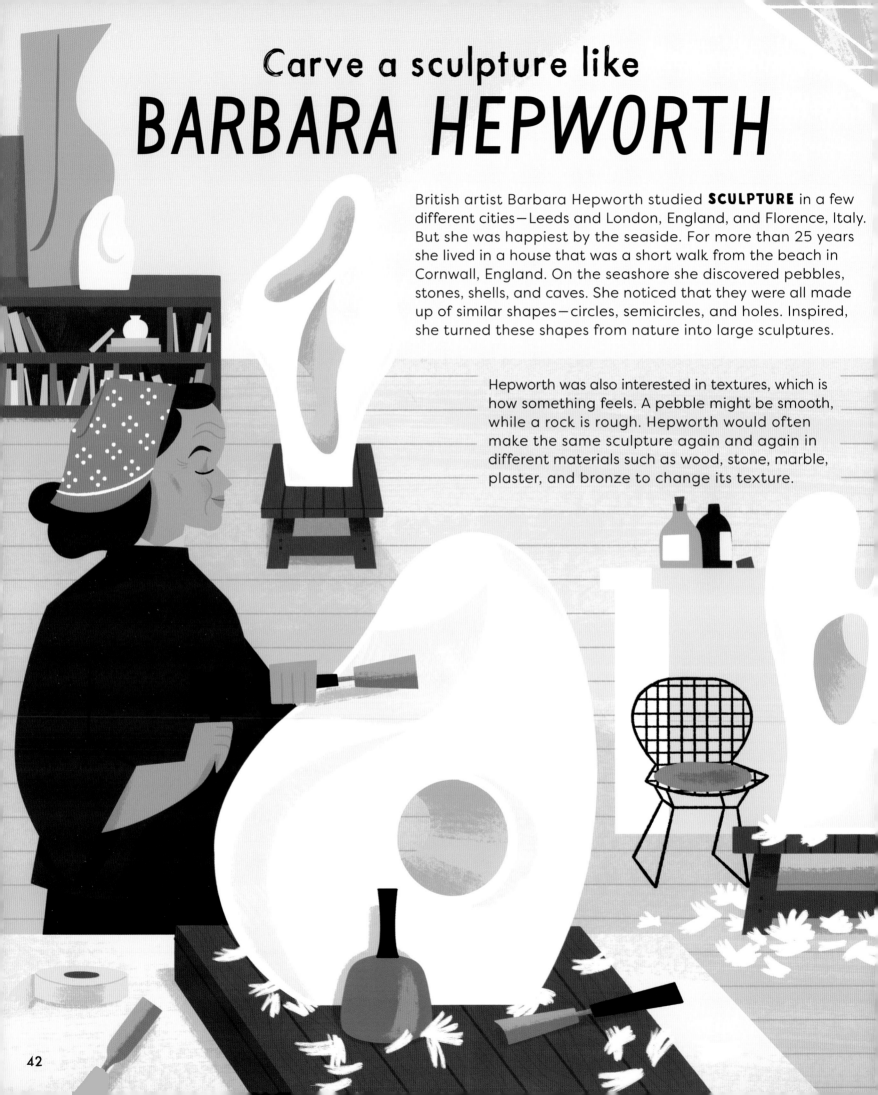

Working with special tools called chisels, Hepworth chipped away and carved into blocks of materials to make her sculptures. While paintings are flat, sculptures are solid three-dimensional objects. This means you can see them from all sides. Hepworth thought people should be able to walk all the way around them. She even invited people to peer through her sculptures by making holes in them.

The holes were just as important as the solid space. Hepworth would leave her finished sculptures outside so it was like peering through a window to another world.

NOW IT'S YOUR TURN!

What you will need:

* A tray (ideally with sides)
* A large bar of soap
* A plastic knife
* A vegetable peeler
* Nail scissors

1 Working on your tray, use a plastic knife or peeler to carve a flat bottom edge on your soap so that it will stand up.

2 Now lay the soap flat. It's time to make holes in it. Pierce where you want your first hole to be with a pair of closed nail scissors. You'll need to ask a grown-up to help with this part.

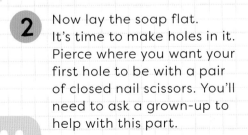

3 Twist and turn the scissors gently until a hole appears. When you break through to the other side of the soap, push the scissors through from the other side. Repeat for each hole you want.

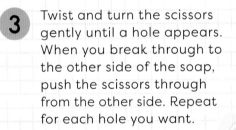

4 You can now use a plastic knife to make the holes wider, working from both sides.

TIP: Make sure the holes are not too close to the edges or each other, because the soap may break.

5 With the peeler, smooth the outer edges of your soap until it's a shape you like. You can smooth it more by dipping your finger in water and running it along the edges. Or you might prefer to leave it rough.

TIP: Why not make a group of soap sculptures of different textures and shapes and exhibit them outside?

Splash paint like
JANET SOBEL

During the 1930s, Ukrainian artist Janet Sobel experimented with painting. Instead of working carefully like many other artists, she would drip, drop, and even throw paint in a messy method, called **DRIP PAINTING**.

In 1908 Sobel moved to New York City, where she had five children with her husband, who made jewelery. She never intended to be an artist, but when her son started art classes, she began to play with his leftover paint and invented her own way of painting.

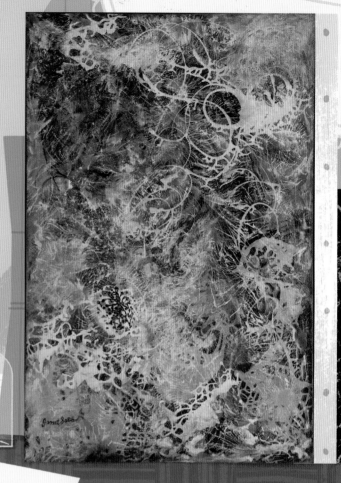

As well as using brushes, she used her husband's jewelery-making tools, including glass pipettes, to drop paint onto scraps of paper.

Soon, Sobel started on huge canvases. Usually, when you look at a painting it's obvious which way up it's supposed to go. But it's much harder to tell which is the top or bottom of Sobel's compositions. That's because she worked on them from all four sides.

NOW IT'S YOUR TURN!

What you will need:

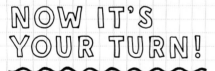
Some sheets of newspaper

The largest piece of white paper you can find (or you can join smaller pieces of paper together with tape on the back)

Sticks, paintbrushes, plastic spoons, chopsticks, and other tools of your choice

Water

Poster paint: black and at least 3 other colors

Some small containers

An apron or overalls (to keep you clean)

1. Place each of your paint colors in a small container (yogurt containers are perfect).

2. Cover the floor with newspaper before placing your big piece of white paper on top of it.

Sobel wasn't interested in making paintings that looked neat or perfect. Instead, she wanted to enjoy the act of making and express herself. "I only paint what I feel," she said. She often listened to music while she painted—it was as if she was dancing with her pictures.

Janet Sobel was the first to make drip paintings like this, but she wasn't the only one. After seeing her work, American artists including Jackson Pollock and his wife Lee Krasner, began to make large pictures by splish-splashing paint to create all-over patterns too.

She would pour, splash, spill, and flick paint in different directions. She would also blow on the paint and even use her vacuum cleaner to drag the paint across the canvas!

3 Stand above your paper with your feet apart. Choose your first tool and use it to drip, splatter, and splash the paint onto the paper below. Start with black, then add one color at a time.

TIP: Be bold with your movements! Wave your hand and arm, flick them up and down, and shake them to add the paint.

4 Move around as you paint, so the paint hits the paper from different directions.

TIP: Put your favorite music on, so you can move while you make your own action painting.

5 Make sure that you have covered the whole paper with paint to give it an all-over quality.

Make pop-art-style prints like
ANDY WARHOL

During the 1960s, American artist Andy Warhol created colorful prints of objects, including cans of soup, bananas, and Coca-Cola bottles. He also made portraits of celebrities, like Elvis Presley and Marilyn Monroe, against bright backgrounds. He was celebrating popular people and products, which is why this type of art is called **POP ART**.

When he lived in New York with his mother, Julia, Warhol had lots of cats—one was named Hester and the others were all named Sam!

He also had a lot of silver wigs. Warhol would often wear them with dark sunglasses and black jackets. He had style and loved to party!

Warhol worked in a building that he called the Factory because he made so much art inside it, including screen prints. He would create a simple design with stencils and ink, such as the outline of a can of soup or large flower, on a screen made of special material. He would then place a piece of paper underneath this screen, pressing down on it to push the ink design through.

Warhol would press the same painted screen onto many different-colored backgrounds. It was an easy way for him to make copies of the same picture, creating a grid of repeated screen prints. With this method, Warhol turned objects from everyday life into fun artworks of different color combinations that 'pop!'

Warhol was a man who loved repetition. He once claimed that he ate the same Campbell's tomato soup every day for lunch for 20 years! You can see Warhol's love for repeating things in his art too.

NOW IT'S YOUR TURN!

What you will need:

A piece of paper

A paintbrush

Poster paint

A halved pepper (or an apple cut in half would also work)

Knife and chopping board

Colored cardstock

A pencil

Scissors

Glue

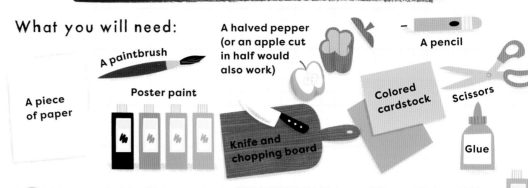

1 Divide a piece of paper into four by folding it in half one way and then the other.

2 Unfold your piece of paper and paint each quarter a different bright color. Let it dry.

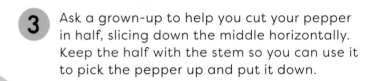

3 Ask a grown-up to help you cut your pepper in half, slicing down the middle horizontally. Keep the half with the stem so you can use it to pick the pepper up and put it down.

4 Lay the cut edge of your halved pepper flat on a piece of colored cardstock. With a pencil, trace around it and then cut it out carefully with scissors. What shape do you see emerging? The outline should look like a flower with four big petals.

5 Repeat this three more times, on different pieces of colored cardstock. You will end up with four different-colored shapes.

6 Once your painted paper is dry, stick each of the four flower-shaped cutouts into the center of the colored sections with glue. Make sure they are all in the same position as one another.

7 It's time to start printing! Dip your pepper into a tray of black paint, making sure the cut edges are covered evenly.

TIP: You could test the printing process before printing onto your colored cardstock.

8 Now press your pepper firmly onto the top of each of the four cut-out shapes, one by one, to create your own pop-art flower prints.

Draw an optical illusion like
BRIDGET RILEY

By painting patterns in clever ways, Riley makes a flat image look like it's jumping off the page. Do you feel dizzy yet?

Bridget Riley is a British artist who wants to amaze your eyes! Her paintings might be flat, but they look like they are moving, with lots of curving, wiggling, and waving lines.

During the 1950s, Riley studied art in London, England. Here she learned about important artists from history, including the French pointillist painter Georges Seurat, who used lots of little dots. Like Seurat, she was interested in how people's eyes see color and shapes.

In the 1960s Riley began to make pictures of patterns, using only black and white lines, circles, and squares. She made it look like her images were flashing and spinning. Later she used different colors in her patterns to confuse people even more.

NOW IT'S YOUR TURN!

1 Draw a large heart on your piece of paper in pencil making it as symmetrical as possible.

2 Place your ruler horizontally about 1 inch below the top edge of the paper and draw a straight line up to the heart, stopping, and continuing the line on the other side.

What you will need:

* A piece of white paper
* A pencil
* A ruler
* A black felt-tip pen
* Two different-colored pencils or crayons

3 Move your ruler down an inch and draw another line. Repeat until you have about eight lines behind the empty heart. Then do the same with vertical lines to make a background of squares.

4 Next, continue the lines inside the heart, but curve them upward and outward.

5 Draw over all the lines with a black felt-tip pen.

6 Color the background squares using two contrasting and alternating colors, such as black and white.

TIP: To help you remember which color needs to fill each square, mark a small dot of color in each section before blocking it in.

7 With the same two colors, fill in the squares inside the heart. Your heart should look like it's popping out off the paper!

Riley's eye-bending art is called **OPTICAL ART** because it's all about optical illusions. These are images that play tricks with your vision. When we look at things, our eyes and brain send messages to each other, but with an optical illusion the complicated colors, lines, and patterns mix up your mind!

Create a crown like
JEAN-MICHEL BASQUIAT

Have you ever seen words or pictures sprayed on walls, windows, or doors? This type of art is called **GRAFFITI** or **STREET ART** because you usually see it on the streets. One of the most important street artists of all time was Jean-Michel Basquiat, who covered his city with colorful pictures of Black people.

Usually he spray-painted pictures of heads, stick figures, skulls, arrows, and crowns.

To paint bold images which stood out when people walked past them, Basquiat would use black and the three bright primary colors—red, blue, and yellow.

During the 1980s, Jean-Michel Basquiat lived in New York City. As a teenager, he was often homeless, which meant he lived and slept on the streets. To make money, he sold T-shirts and postcards he designed himself.

He also used cans of spray paint to create street art across the city. He didn't want it to look neat or perfect. Instead, it was supposed to look like a child had drawn it.

He sometimes painted on walls near big museums and art galleries, so important people working in them could see his art. They were very impressed because it was so different to the paintings they had inside the museums and, soon, they asked him to make graffiti pictures they could include in their exhibitions.

Basquiat, who was very happy to be asked, spray-painted the images of Black men, including jazz musicians, athletes and writers, onto paper. He wanted to celebrate other people who looked like him.

A crown is a symbol of someone special and by giving his Black male figures their own crowns, Basquiat showed them as heroes, saints, or royals.

NOW IT'S YOUR TURN!

What you will need:

* A piece of cardboard from a cereal box or package
* A pencil
* Scissors
* Some newspaper
* A tape measure or ruler
* Poster paint
* An empty spray bottle (This could be an old cleaning product, but make sure it's completely clean before you use it.)
* Oil pastels
* A paintbrush
* A hole punch
* Two strips of ribbon

1 With a pencil, draw the outline of your crown onto a piece of cardboard. Make sure it has three tall peaks and is wide enough for your head.

TIP: Use a tape measure, ruler, or strip of ribbon to measure the width of your head from one ear to the other.

2 Cut out your crown and lay it on some newspaper.

3 Unscrew the nozzle of an old spray bottle and add a small amount of yellow paint. Then mix in plenty of water to turn it into a runny liquid.

4 Aim the nozzle at your cardboard crown and spray your paint at it.

5 Once the paint is dry, add red and blue scribbles with oil pastels. Create a thin black outline around the edges of the crown.

6 Use a hole punch (or ask a grown-up to use scissors) to make two holes on either side of the crown. Thread a long strip of ribbon through each of the two holes and knot them in place. Tie the ribbon around your head and wear your Basquiat crown with pride!

Wrap a string sculpture like
JUDITH SCOTT

American artist Judith Scott was deaf and never learned to speak. But she could use art to express herself. In the 1980s, she began to make sculptures by wrapping different objects in string, ribbons, yarn, and other pieces of fabric.

Scott had Down's Syndrome and, at age seven, she was sent away to a school for disabled children and separated from her twin sister, Joyce. But once her sister was a grown-up she decided to take care of Scott herself, later sending her to a class where she could learn about art.

For two years, Scott showed no interest in making anything. But one day a new teacher showed the group how to make sculptures using twigs, branches, and string. This is called **FIBER ART**. Scott, then 43, was captivated. She immediately started to wrap twigs with yarn and the other materials that the teacher had brought with her.

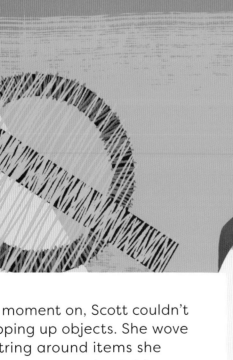

From this moment on, Scott couldn't stop wrapping up objects. She wove colorful string around items she found in her home and outside on the streets—keys, shopping carts, chairs, bicycle wheels, and broomsticks. She would cover them with so many layers you could no longer see what was underneath!

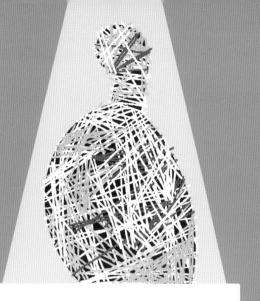

Some sculptures took Scott weeks, or even months, to finish. Once completed, she would wave at her artworks or pat them gently like they were her friends.

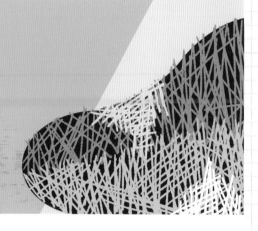

She even covered herself in ribbons, scarves, and fabric to create sculptures of her own head!

Although Scott only started making art as an adult, today her sculptures can be seen in museums and galleries around the world, showing that it's never too late to become an artist.

NOW IT'S YOUR TURN!

What you will need:

A roll of toilet paper

Scissors

Different-colored string, ribbons, yarn, and other fabrics

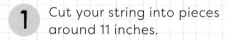

1 Cut your string into pieces around 11 inches.

2 Cut six small snips into each end of the toilet paper roll, spacing them equally.

3 Take your first piece of string and tuck the end of it into one of the slits. Wrap it around and around the toilet paper roll in different directions. Once you come to the end of the string, tuck it into another one of the slits.

4 Repeat this with your next piece of string.

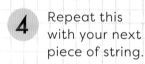

TIP: Tie pieces of string together or weave them under and over each other.

5 Keep going until you think it looks finished. When it's complete you could give it a friendly wave or pat it.

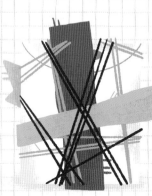

Wash over wax like
EMILY KAME KNGWARREYE

Born in 1910, Emily Kame Kngwarreye is one of Australia's most important Aboriginal artists. Working outside in the sunshine, she made art that was all about the huge, hot desert that she came from. Her paintings were also about her very special name.

Kngwarreye's beautiful batik designs, filled with lines and dots, were based on what she saw in the bush: the sun, stars, lizards, snakes, and plants.

Aboriginal people were the first people who lived in Australia. For thousands of years Kngwarreye's ancestors survived in remote areas filled with rocks, red earth, tall grass, and wildflowers. This type of landscape is called the bush.

Because Aboriginal people lived off the land, some were given traditional names after special areas or plants in their homelands. Kngwarreye's was 'Kame'—this refers to the yam, a potato-like plant.

NOW IT'S YOUR TURN!

What you will need:

Poster paint

A white wax crayon or a thin white candle

A piece of thick white paper or cardstock

Yogurt containers

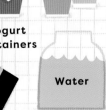

Water

A thick paintbrush

1. With your crayon or the flat end of a candle, draw an animal in the center of your piece of paper or cardstock, pressing down firmly. Leave some space around it to decorate the page with dots and lines.

TIP: It may be hard to see your animal on the white paper, so work near a bright light or window.

During the 1970s, Kngwarreye learned to make art using a technique called **BATIK**. Working outside, she would take a piece of silk or cotton and stretch it over her knees.

Next, she would pour hot wax over her fabric in designs of her choice. She would then add special dyes that would stick everywhere except where the wax was, creating a painted pattern.

When she was older Kngwarreye also began to make pictures with acrylic paint, using colors from the hot desert bush and sky—red, yellow, and blue. Like her batik designs, these are filled with dotted and overlapping lines. Some look like animal tracks, plants, and seeds, while others look like maps of the land or drops of rain. Many also look like the tangled roots of the yam plant—Kngwarreye was painting pictures to reflect her country and cultural knowledge.

2 In yogurt containers, mix two or three poster paint colors with water until they are very watery.

3 Using a thick paintbrush, add your first color to the paper, focusing on the area around your animal.

4 Do the same around the edges of your paper with your second and third colors, one color at a time.

Once dry, you'll have a batik picture like Kngwarreye!

Turn yourself invisible like
LIU BOLIN

Even though artists all make different work—from small sculptures to giant paintings—they always create something that you can *see*. But Liu Bolin, better known as "the Invisible Man," does the exact opposite. He covers his own body in paint to blend into various backgrounds, hiding himself in cities around the world.

Born in 1973, contemporary Chinese artist Bolin started his career by making sculptures from his studio in the big city of Beijing. But in 2005 this studio was destroyed to make room for a new building for the 2008 Olympic Games. Bolin felt like he, an artist, was not important, so he decided to make himself vanish.

He painted his body white and gray, like the dusty rubble, and stood in front of the broken stones for many hours. This type of art, where people perform actions with their own bodies, is called **PERFORMANCE ART**.

Using make-up and paint on his clothes, shoes, and body, Bolin creates a camouflage—like an animal that uses color as a disguise to help it to hide. It means he is hard to see because he matches the environment.

It takes "the invisible man" hours and sometimes several days, to create his cunning camouflage. He has "disappeared" against walls of graffiti in New York City, beside ancient statues in the city of Pompeii, and in front of soft toys in a Disney store. With this great game of hide-and-seek, Bolin is inviting you to look closer at the world, searching for things, people, and animals that might be hard to see.

NOW IT'S YOUR TURN!

▼▼▼▼▼▼▼

What you will need:

White paper

Poster paint

A paintbrush

A pencil

1 Choose an animal print, such as zebra stripes or leopard spots, and sketch out the pattern on a piece of paper. Fill the entire page.

2 With your paintbrush and paint, carefully color in the pattern and let it dry. Work with one color at a time and remember to clean your brush in between colors.

3 Now it's time to camouflage yourself! With your paintbrush and paint, decorate your hand with the same pattern—make sure you paint the same size stripes or spots.

4 Once you have finished painting your hand, place it over the paper. Is it camouflaged?

TIP: You could also take a photo of your performance art.

TIP: Test a small amount of paint on a finger first to make sure you don't have an allergic reaction.

Make a polka-dot pumpkin like YAYOI KUSAMA

Since she was a very young child, Japanese artist Yayoi Kusama has painted with polka dots. She covers paintings, drawings, sculptures, and even her own clothes in them! But why is she so dotty about dots?

Kusama was born in 1929 in the Japanese town, Matsumoto. Her family made money by growing flowers and selling their seeds all over Japan, so her house was surrounded by meadows and greenhouses filled with plants.

Every day Kusama sat outside and painted pictures in her sketchbook. These early works were filled with dots because she saw circles all around her—in the fields of flowers, as well as the sun and moon in the sky.

Kusama remembers that one day the flowers started talking to her and, once, when she went to pick a large pumpkin with her grandfather, it began speaking to her.

Although she was scared by these strange experiences, which we call hallucinations, she kept drawing as a way of coping with what she saw and felt. When Kusama was around 17 or 18, she drew a picture of a pumpkin which won her a prize in a competition. Since then, Kusama has continued to paint and sculpt pumpkins and flowers, covering them with bright polka dots and exhibiting them in gallery spaces all over the world. This is known as **INSTALLATION ART**.

NOW IT'S YOUR TURN!

1 Cover one piece of cardstock with large polka dots, drawing them in pencil and coloring them in with crayon.

What you will need:

★ **Two pieces of cardstock**
★ **A pencil**
★ **Crayons**
★ **Scissors**
★ **Glue or tape**

2 Cut your piece of dotty cardstock into eight long equal strips.

TIP: You can color the dots the same color or different colors—it's up to you.

3 On your second piece of cardstock, draw two circles and cut them out. You could draw around a mug for size.

4 Stick the eight strips to one of the circles. First make a cross shape through the center, then add the remaining pieces in between the lines of the cross in a star shape.

5 Starting with the center cross, curl the strips up and around one at a time, and stick them onto the second circle. You will now have a 3D pumpkin shape.

Kusama once said that "Polka dots can't stay alone," so she always paints many spots in all different colors.

6 Cut out a small rectangle from the leftover cardstock. Fold one end over to create a small flap around 1/2 inch long and stick this to the top of your pumpkin to create a stem.

Make a mural like
ESTHER MAHLANGU

South African artist Dr. Esther Mahlangu began painting at the age of 10. Instead of working inside on small pieces of paper or cardstock, she was outside, covering the walls of houses in her village with colorful patterns.

In the 1940s, Mahlangu was taught to paint by her mother and grandmother, who belong to the Ndebele people who live in South Africa. For over 100 years, Ndebele women have used paint and cow dung to decorate the outside of their homes.

Mahlangu remembers that when she first started to paint **MURALS** she was told to practice on the back of the house because it would not be seen by many people. But over time she proved she had a great talent and moved to the front of the house.

NOW IT'S YOUR TURN!

What you will need:

A pencil

A ruler

A piece of white paper or cardstock

Black and colored felt-tip pens

1 With a pencil draw an equal border round all four sides of your paper.

TIP: An easy way to do this is to use the width of a ruler.

2 Fill this border with a pattern of repeating shapes. Try to make sure the pattern is symmetrical.

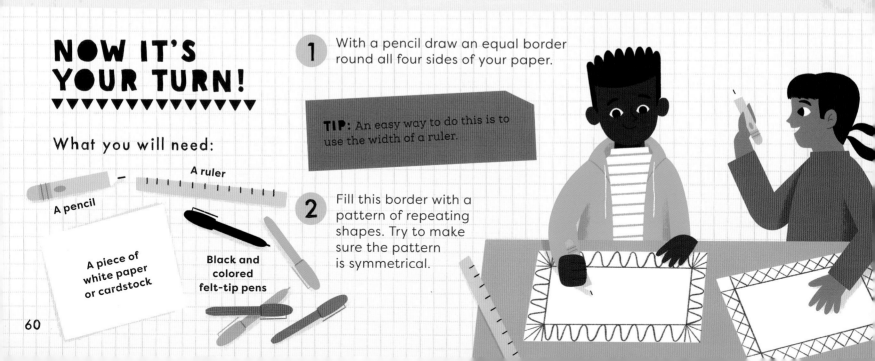

People would stop and stare at Mahlangu's massive murals. Each of them is made of patterns—lines, shapes, and colors repeated again and again. Many of her patterns are also symmetrical, which means if you drew a line down the middle, it would look the same on both sides.

Mahlangu's designs also have lots of straight black lines. Mahlangu doesn't use a ruler though—she learned through many years of practice to keep her hand steady as she draws and paints.

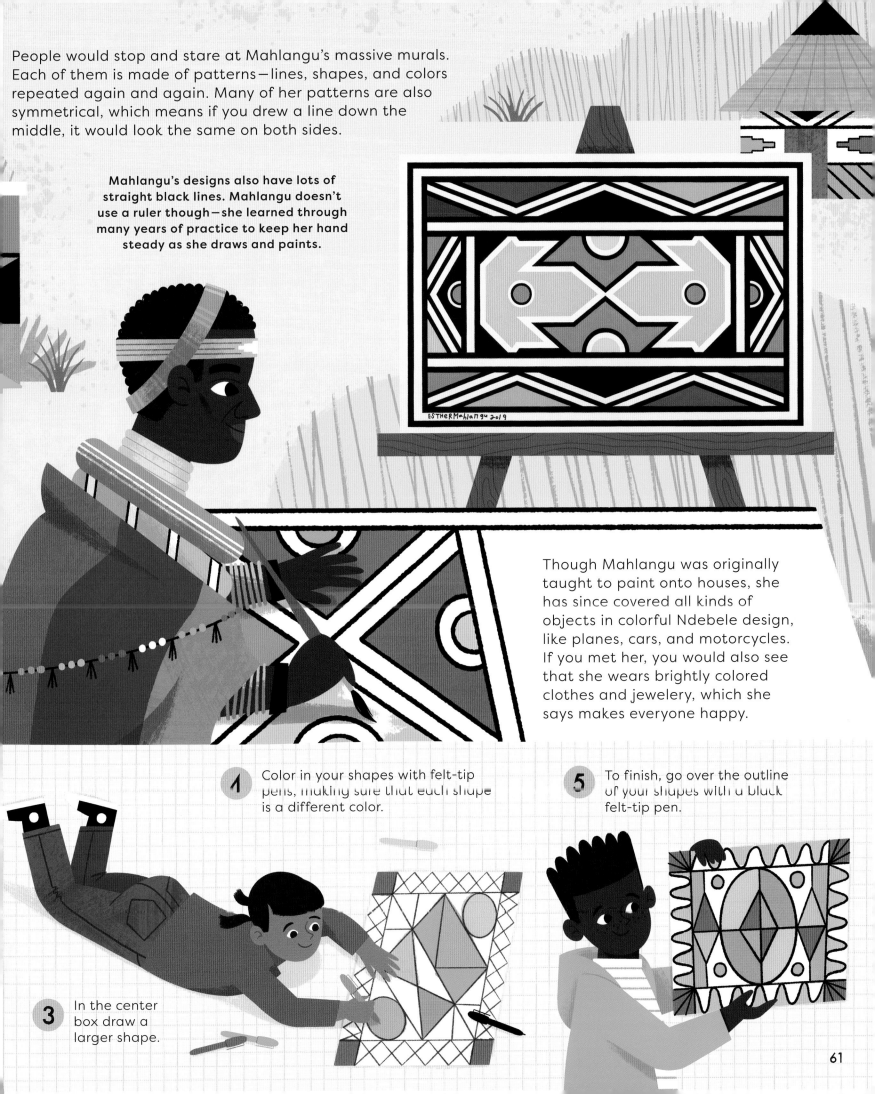

ESTHERMahlangu 2019

Though Mahlangu was originally taught to paint onto houses, she has since covered all kinds of objects in colorful Ndebele design, like planes, cars, and motorcycles. If you met her, you would also see that she wears brightly colored clothes and jewelery, which she says makes everyone happy.

4 Color in your shapes with felt-tip pens, making sure that each shape is a different color.

5 To finish, go over the outline of your shapes with a black felt-tip pen.

3 In the center box draw a larger shape.

GLOSSARY

ABSTRACT A style of art made up of lines, shapes, and colors, rather than representing a person or object.

ANATOMY The study of human body parts, inside and out.

ARTIST Anyone who makes art!

ART MOVEMENT When a group of artists use the same style or subject in their work.

BACKGROUND The part of a picture that is furthest away from you.

CANVAS A type of pale cloth that artists paint on.

CARVE To cut into the surface of a stone, piece of wood, or other material to make a new shape.

CAVE PAINTING A picture on a cave wall or ceiling, usually painted thousands of years ago.

CHISEL A sharp tool used to carve a sculpture.

COLLAGE A picture made from sticking down different materials, such as cardstock and paper, with glue.

COLOR WHEEL A tool that shows artists which colors work well next to one another and how to mix them together.

COMPLEMENTARY COLOR A color that makes another color stand out more, for example, red makes green look greener.

COMPOSITION How different parts of an artwork, including shapes and colors, are arranged.

CUBISM A style of art where an object or person is made up of lines and shapes, including cubes.

DADA A type of art and poetry made by chance and meant to break the rules.

DRIP PAINTING A style of art made by dripping, splashing, and pouring paint.

EXPERIMENT To try out new ideas, methods and styles. Some of the best art is made by experimenting!

FIBER ART A style of art using objects made from yarn, string, and other soft materials.

FOREGROUND The part of a picture that is closest to you.

GRAFFITI Writing or drawings spray painted on surfaces (most often outside walls).

HORIZONTAL LINE A straight line drawn from right to left, or left to right.

IMPRESSIONISM A style of art made to capture light, colors and an artist's "impression" of a scene, often using lots of small brushstrokes.

INSTALLATION ART Art made for, and put inside, a specific space.

INVISIBLE Something you can't see.

LANDSCAPE An artwork that shows natural scenery, such as gardens, mountains, and rivers.

MEASURE To find out how long or wide something is, often by using a ruler.

MOSAIC Art made from sticking down lots of tiny tiles, arranged in a pattern.

MURAL A large painting made on a wall or ceiling.

MUSEUM A building that houses, displays, and takes care of objects, including artworks.

OPTICAL ILLUSION An image that plays tricks on your eyes and mind.

OUTLINE A line drawn around the edge of a main shape.

PALETTE A flat board that an artist can hold in one hand and mix their paint colors on.

PATTERN Shapes, colors, and lines that are repeated on a surface.

POINTILLISM A style of art made from tiny points of pure color placed next to one another to create a picture.

POP ART A style of art based on colorful pictures of popular, everyday items, including cans of soup, bottles, or bananas.

PORTRAIT A painting, drawing, photograph, or sculpture of a person.

POST-IMPRESSIONISM Made after Impressionism, a style of art to express an artist's thoughts, emotions, and feelings.

PRIMARY COLOR A color that can't be mixed from other colors. The 3 primary colors are red, yellow, and blue.

PRINT To make copies of the same picture using the same materials again and again.

PROPORTIONS The length and distance between parts of a body or object.

SCULPTURE Three-dimensional, solid art objects made from stone, clay, wood, or other materials.

SECONDARY COLOR A color made by mixing two primary colors together.

SELF-PORTRAIT An artist's picture of themselves.

SILHOUETTE A line drawn around an object, person, animal, or scene filled with a single color, usually black.

SPIRAL A curved shape that starts in the middle and goes around and around.

STILL LIFE A work of art showing objects that are motionless, like apples or flowers.

STREET ART A style of art made from pictures and signs sprayed on outside walls.

STUDIO A space where an artist works and keeps their materials.

STYLE The way an artwork looks.

SURREALISM A style of art based on dreams and the imagination, rather than real life.

SYMMETRICAL Something that looks the same on both sides.

TECHNIQUE How an artwork is made.

TEXTURE How something feels, for example, whether it is rough or smooth.

THREE-DIMENSIONAL (3D) A shape with three dimensions — length, width, and depth. It is not flat like a two-dimensional shape.

TRACE To copy a shape by drawing around it or pressing down from one piece of paper onto another.

VERTICAL LINE A straight line drawn from down to up, or up to down.

VIBRANT Brightly colored.

ABOUT THE AUTHOR AND ILLUSTRATOR

RUTH MILLINGTON is an art historian and author who writes about amazing artists of the past and present. She has written for national newspapers and appeared on TV and radio, telling stories about Surrealism, Vincent van Gogh, and Frida Kahlo, among others. Her first adult art book, *Muse*, uncovers the real-life people featured in famous portraits. Ruth also loves to read, sing, paint, and decorate her home with lots and lots of art!

ELLEN SURREY is an illustrator out of sunny Los Angeles, California. Blending her love of mid-century design and vintage children's books, Ellen enjoys finding beauty in the past and colorfully sharing it with a contemporary audience. Her work has appeared in many newspapers and she's illustrated many books about inspirational people, including Dolly Parton! When she isn't working, Ellen enjoys watching old movies and visiting her favorite thrift stores.

ACKNOWLEDGEMENTS

Thanks to Tina García, Victoria England, Jo Jordan, Allison Hill, and the rest of the Nosy Crow team for making this book happen. Thanks also to Claire Guest, Jennie Roman, and Emma Young for their invaluable help.

The publisher would like to thank the copyright holders for granting permission to use the following copyright material:
Page 12: *GuaTewett Tree of Life* © Luc-Henri Fage / English Wikipedia, 1999. **Page 15**: "Cave canem" mosaic from Pompeii, Casa di Orfeo. By permission of the Ministry of Culture—National Archaeological Museum of Naples—photo by Giorgio Albano. **Page 16:** Leonardo da Vinci, *Vitruvian Man*, 1490 © Gallerie dell'Accademia di Venezia. **Page 18:** Artemisia Gentileschi, *Self-portrait as the Allegory of Painting (La Pittura)*, 1638-9. © Royal Collection / Royal Collection Trust © Her Majesty Queen Elizabeth II, 2022 / Bridgeman Images. **Page 21:** Katsushika Hokusai, *Under the Wave off Kanagawa*, 1830-32. The Metropolitan Museum of Art, New York, H. O. Havemeyer Collection, Bequest of Mrs. H. O. Havemeyer, 1929. **Page 23:** Moses Williams, *Revealed Silhouette of a Young Woman*, aftcr 1802 © Muscum of Fine Arts, IIouston / The Bayou Bend Collection, gift of Miss Ima Hogg / Bridgeman Images. **Page 25:** Claude Monet, *The Water Lily Pond*, 1899 © 2022 The Metropolitan Museum of Art / Art Resource NY / Scala Florence. **Page 26:** Georges Seurat, *A Sunday on La Grande Jatte*, 1884/86. The Art Institute of Chicago. **Page 28:** Vincent Van Gogh, *Vase With Three Sunflowers*, 1888. Private Collection. Photo © Steeve E. Flowers. / Alamy Stock Photo. **Page 30:** Henri Matisse, *The Snail*, 1953 Photo: © Tate. Artwork: © Succession H. Matisse / DACS 2023. **Page 32:** Pablo Picasso, *Table in a Cafe, Bottle of Pernod*, 1912. The State Hermitage Museum, St. Petersburg. Photograph © The State Hermitage Museum / photo by Vladimir Terebenin. © Succession Picasso / DACS, London 2022. **Page 35:** Hilma af Klint, *The Ten Largest, No. 3. Youth*, 1907 © Hilma af Klint Foundation. **Page 36:** Salvador Dalí, *The Persistence of Memory*, 1931 © Salvador Dalí, Fundació Gala-Salvador Dalí, DACS 2022. Martin Shields / Alamy Stock Photo. **Page 38**: Frida Kahlo, *Self-portrait with Hummingbird and Thorn Necklace*, 1940 © Banco de México Diego Rivera Frida Kahlo Museums Trust, Mexico, D. F. / DACS 2022. Photo Martin Shields / Alamy Stock Photo. **Page 40:** Hugo Ball, *Karawane*, 1916. User Albrecht Conz on de.wikipedia, Public domain, via Wikimedia Commons. **Page 43:** Barbara Hepworth, *The Family of Man*, 1970 © Bowness. Photo: geogphotos / Alamy Stock Photo. **Page 44:** Janet Sobel (1894-1968): *Milky Way*, 1945. Enamel on canvas, 7/8 x 29 7/8" (114 x 75.9 cm). Gift of the artist's family. New York, Museum of Modern Art (MoMA) © 2022. Digital image, The Museum of Modern Art, New York / Scala, Florence. **Page 47:** Andy Warhol, *Green Marilyn*, Andy Warhol, 1962 © 2022 The Andy Warhol Foundation for the Visual Arts, Inc. / Licensed by DACS, London. Photo Martin Shields / Alamy Stock Photo. **Page 48:** Bridget Riley, *Untitled (Diagonal Curve)*, 1966 © Bridget Riley 2022. All rights reserved. **Page 51:** Jean-Michel Basquiat, *Untitled*, 1982 © The Estate of Jean-Michel Basquiat / ADAGP, Paris and DACS, London 2022. Photo © Christie's Images / Bridgeman Images. **Page 52:** Judith Scott, *Untitled 2004*. Courtesy of Judith Scott and Creative Growth Art Center. **Page 54:** Emily Kame Kngwarreye, *Untitled (Alhalkere)*, 1981 © Emily Kame Kngwarreye / Copyright Agency. Licensed by DACS 2022. **Page 57:** Courtesy of Liu Bolin and Liu Bolin Art Studio. **Page 58:** Yayoi Kusama, *Pumpkin 2013* © YAYOI KUSAMA. **Page 61:** Esther Mahlangu, *Ndebele Abstract*, 2019 © The Melrose Gallery. Every effort has been made to obtain permission to reproduce copyright material, but there may have been cases where we have been unable to trace a copyright holder. The publisher would be happy to correct any omissions in future printings.